Infragreen

by the same author

Cohabitation
Quicksand Beach

Infragreen
Kate Bingham

SEREN

Seren is the book imprint of
Poetry Wales Press Ltd.
57 Nolton Street, Bridgend, Wales, CF31 3AE
www.serenbooks.com
facebook.com/SerenBooks
twitter@SerenBooks

© Kate Bingham 2015
ISBN: 978-1-78172-243-5
e-book: 978-1-78172-245-9
Kindle: 978-1-78172-244-2

A CIP record for this title is available from the British Library.

The publisher acknowledges the financial assistance of the Welsh Books Council.

Cover Image: 'The Fruit' by Paul Klee, 1932.

Printed in Bembo by Bell & Bain Ltd, Glasgow.

Author website: www.katebingham.com

Contents

I

II

III

I

Ultragreen

A water drop
turns in its skin at the end of the garden
and opens one eye to the sun.

Unsteadily, at the speed of light, its plain
no-coloured heart breaks into such a green I can hear it
loud and bright and green to distraction.

It turns its eye in my brain, looks out
and sees what I have seen.
Something like photosynthesis begins.

Infragreen

Something the sun and I see eye to eye in
winks in the crux of a leaf.

For every turn of the turning earth
it makes a tiny correction

half letting go of itself
half hanging on.

Spring

You know what the sun is like
it has a way of looking at us from side to side

of rising above its various nationalities
and making things grow

as if that's what a life-form has to do
to get more attention.

Up come snow drops
pushing and shoving and putting on weight

daffodil nubs break out all at once
where the grass is thin

and even the weak municipal crocuses
divide and multiply, insisting they matter.

An empty plastic milk container
left on the kitchen table

takes a breath, increasing in volume
filling with light.

look at the rain   it always seems to know what to do
coming down clear and direct   silver and fearless
many too many to count   in one quick freshwater shoal
no thought   no thought at all   for what happens next

shaped by the air it runs through going its absolute fastest
round at one end   sharp at the other   in and out of control
it manages somehow to look its best   its every last drop
clean and true and hurrying to put its foot in its footstep

falling over itself into earth's cracked bowl
it disappears as it collects   vanishing from the pavement up
grounding the sky and lifting filthy waters
falling into itself in the street as if only falling matters

On Highgate Hill

How it rained;
we caught the bus up Highgate Hill
past Whittington's cat and the hospital.
The driver insisted he was full –
twenty wet children, pleading, shrill,
    how it rained.

How it snowed;
the bus got stuck on Highgate Hill
and we stood on the pavement in pumps and heels,
children pelted the windows and wheels,
their walk to school a wild white thrill,
    how it snowed.

How it shone;
we held our breath down Highgate Hill
through stinking heat. A teenage girl
chucked study guides across the aisle,
a boy spat on Swiss Army steel
    and it shone,

how it shone;
the children kicked their seats until
the driver came roaring up out of his stall.
He bent in the middle. We saw it all.
The engine turned over. Traffic stood still.
    How it shone.

Silt

Between the school and Whitehill Food Market
two small motor repair shops operate
from opposite sides of the street, one on the corner,
one with Hand Car Wash And Valet Services
sharing its neat white stucco art deco yard,
where less than once a year I take the car
to have its moss scraped off and some of the silt
sucked out of the velvet-effect upholstery,
sugar and salt and worms of rubbed white tissue,
anonymous embedded grime, filaments
and particles of inner-city filth
accumulated through the ins and outs
of all those journeys, prints of my footprints pressed
on the brake like a prehistoric assemblage,
the padded bodywork a safe, repulsive
five-seater cave I have to return to,
part of the landscape, its familiar volume
somewhere to look from as a dirty sun
slides behind chimneys and rooftops, or the moon
comes out from a billboard, centring the sky
between Whitehill Food Market and the school,
where a glade of plane trees reaches over the fence
of the padlocked playground and a broken drain
wells at the side of the street in long black water,
sluicing the pavement, falling back on itself
and sluicing again as cars slow through ahead
of the traffic island, washing a black sand beach
inland over glittery concrete flood plains
to the walls of houses no one seems to occupy,
leaving a line of scribbled minuscule trash,
the loose-packed stinking edge of a continent.

The World at One

I lie in bed until *The World at One,*
why should my heart go off with an alarm?
The body's woman's work is never done,

the blood gets up to exercise the lungs.
The kettle sings, I count my lucky charms –
a chain connects and separates each one

and when I shake my wrist it shakes the sun
that scatters off the wall and scalds my arm.
It's only skin and coffee, no harm done.

War continues, voting has begun;
my left-hand thumb elects my right-hand palm.
We couldn't all go on to be someone.

I have a little silver house to run,
a silver Scottie dog to keep me calm.
I don't remember everything I've done

but bring me pencil, paper, chewing gum
and I will stay at home and do no harm,
imagining myself a world for one
where what I did was what I should have done.

Heels

High over dogs and tricycles at the gate
I carried myself like wine in a wine glass

managing to avoid the usual huddles
of mums and dads

as instep to instep *left* and *right*
admired their patent leather reflections

proud and voluptuous still
after years in a box at the back of the wardrobe.

Nothing I had to celebrate but the shoes themselves
could account for such inappropriate footwear

and as I sank into the playground's spongy pink tarmac
even the littlest children knew it.

Tulips

My love arrived with tulips, 'ten for a fiver',
picked up from the supermarket at the end of the street.

Fresh off the plane, perhaps he would have preferred
to wash his hands but stood in his coat in the kitchen

watching me slice through cellophane
and crush the stems with the stainless heel of the bread knife.

All across Holland trucks were going to and fro
between the flower farms and distribution facilities

rocking their harvest to sleep over good Dutch tarmac
so every bunch could be in store before it opened its eyes

and even as I filled the vase, people on nights
were dumping crates of slender-headed replacements

cut so premature they didn't know what kind they were
in tubs of glucose solution up and down Holloway Road.

Soon these too would speak the international language of flowers
and be the thing someone can't find the words to say

carrying on with the business of tulips, ripening through
the colourful inconvenience of their visit

into a blousy, brittle, burnt black-burgundy arrangement
of decay, like mine, too tongue-twisted to throw out.

Arrangements

I

I let my best-laid plans be rearranged,
my point of view is narrow and pragmatic:
for things to stay the same they have to change.

I listen to the people I estrange.
I'm insincere, they say, too diplomatic.
Once they liked the world my words arranged

but now they find my argument restrained,
my thought provisional and undogmatic.
No one hears when I explain that change

is necessary, just as truth is strange
and adaptation rarely democratic.
To keep ahead, one must extend one's range.

My family suspects I am deranged.
Insanity could not be less dramatic:
to stay the same a person has to change.

Survival is a complicated game
that disadvantages the bureaucratic;
all my promises are prearranged
to break, should certain circumstances change.

II

I will not tell you what I have arranged
but promise this: I only seem pragmatic.
Let their circumstances stay the same

and people will have reason to complain.
My insincerity is diplomatic;
revolutions need to be arranged,

protest stimulated and contained.
History applauds the undogmatic
but, to change, we have to stay the same.

All my relationships are under strain.
My critics wish I were more democratic,
they want everything to be arranged

around the give-and-take of praise and blame,
but compromise will not provoke dramatic
change. The status quo must stay the same.

When there is fighting in the streets again
my point of view will look less bureaucratic.
Wait, and see the old world rearranged.
For things to change they have to stay the same.

Rosa *Wedding Day*

More than a thousand buds have arrived in the garden.
Yesterday I looked and there were none.

Tangled into a slump of sullen green
and bursting with sap they've overrun

the armandii buddleia jasmine vine
and cluster by cluster flick their swollen thumbs

or sit on their fingers waiting to open,
point their beaks up at the little sun.

Their copper thorns will not be soft for long
and something like a feather in a lung

unfurls its spine inside their inside skin.
A feeling wonders what it might become

as daylight budges up, slips in between
as if there were enough for every one.

Rain or shine they will be flowers soon
and by their own extravagant over-production

lost in a scented commotion of white then gone:
hips where their heads were, this year's growing done.

The rose will forget its name but ramble on
with a fence in its shoulder, rubbing its bones, unstrung.

The sky remembers everything it's seen.
More than a thousand buds stick out their tongues.

At Night

I take the little pill I take at night.
In strips of 21 as flat and white
as faces in the bathroom mirror light
it waits behind the mirror out of sight.
Its days are plastic-coated, watertight,
and all, until the day the day is right,
some sharp or softer shade of dull or bright.

The sun goes in and out but every night
no matter if the day was blue or white
I catch myself in the electric light.
I can't intend an act of oversight.
I tie a ponytail and pull it tight.
I know the pill is perfectly alright
(its documented side-effects are slight)

but wake up with a question in the night
or sometimes keep its sweet dissolving white
on my tongue long after turning off the light,
just as the moon keeps me in line of sight
although the blind is drawn, the curtain tight,
imagining an answer, mine and right
and unconditional as stars are bright.

Questions

How I have grown to love watching you
not answer questions

your openly uninformative eyes
your inadmissible forehead, figured brow
and chin's obscure intelligence

the in and out deliberation of your breath
your steady hand, your other hand

your mouth's unstated strategy
for the avoidance of speech
the generous glue that sets your lips apart

your tongue's invertebrate mobility
dusk pink in the black of your throat

the black of your voice box, fitted as standard
still to be found, still signalling a wish
upon its own red light

the possibility that somewhere
in the processes of deep non-verbal reasoning

some filament might signal back
and the silence between us
end in words.

Midnight

I have had too much sleep to sleep
but not enough to let me keep
tomorrow's promises and lie
awake all night. Instead of sheep

I count the faint familiar sighs
of taxi drivers passing by.
I wonder if they've lost their way,
the roads are hard to recognise –

even our own – the houses sway
in light-polluted pavement grey.
Your breath is seasonless and slow
as aeroplanes at break of day

and when I hear your step below
my heart gets up to meet you, though
you're here with me asleep, I know,
and haven't anywhere to go.

two of us awake in the dark   at least not sleeping
as the morning's first soft notes poke out their pale green shoots

a line of cracks of light
so like a line from birdsong they must be birdsong

lifting its head for an in-breath   shoulders opening into wings

its flutter of pitch a quick explosion in my ear
where a pear tree stands with its hands out hoping for music

and two small thoughts keep still on a branch in the streetlight
one listening   one listening to itself

II

Open

The sound of the place was the sound of summer air –
on holiday the same place every year
it was a field or tree or temperature
I never thought to hear and never heard

until the time I took a boy up there
and closed his eyes and with his open ear
my prickled lips and cheeks and forehead saw
behind the sun the singing of a bird.

If I had never listened to a heart
till then, I would have felt the sudden shame
and same unfolding lunatic delight

I felt beneath that fluttering spark in flight,
discovering the lark and in its name
a song that had been with me from the start.

The Children's Room

for Mum and Dad

You gave us the warmest room in the house
and a pair of old iron frame hospital beds
we'd jump between in our dressing gowns,
pounding the beams in the kitchen below as we landed,
louder and faster each summer holidays
till the cracks in the skirting filled with light
and the sound of grown-ups rattling cutlery
and chairs tucked under for the night
lullabied through the floorboards. We could hear
every creak, every whisper, even the dust
in the background where you dozed on the sofa,
face to the ceiling, eyes half shut.
World going on as it would with us not there
was a world we could sleep through.
Half a life later, nothing has changed up here:
flower-men holding hands still nod and bow
in the wallpaper, bedsteads lean,
and the same pyjama-striped horsehair mattresses
scrunch under candlewick counterpanes
when the children climb in, upping their voices,
clamouring to be kissed. How quickly quietness
comes back to a house after the noise of bedtime
as I chop an onion, open wine,
sit down, slip out of earshot, out of mind.

String

The farmer kept his trousers up with string.
Out of his pockets like an entertainer
with a Punch and Judy sausage-string
he summoned knots of orange binder twine,
a scruffy scratchy plastic nest of string
his filthy freckled hands pressed into mine.

The lining of his jacket hung in strings
but there would be a Cadbury's Eclair,
a humbug, or a coil of licorice string
unwinding somewhere, hidden in the hem,

and I was not to give him back his string
until his fingers turned into a hen
and laid a sweet. He didn't need the string,
I tugged his arm and trotted after him.

Strip

Where they grew wheat, the field crammed full of it,
so thick not even a careful child could creep
between the spiky hedgerow and the crop
without angering the farmer, now a fence
runs up to the tree on the hill, the land is split
and over our little strip weeds compete
for the earth's last goodness – thistles I know I topped
in May, back again and flowering with a vengeance.

All that ridiculous shouldering of rusty blades
when pesticide would have done the job instead
and left no survivors! Blisters couldn't stop me.
I chopped and slashed till it was thistle-free,
the farmer pleased, the grass an even green
display of time and energy well wasted.

Ten O'Clock

        and rooks are still beating in from the barley field,
ones and twos of them, spilling their voices and rolling their wings
in a quick black blur through charcoal twilight,
last quick things of the day beating over the treetops
and into my eye at full stretch.

Only green can bear to drain this slowly out of a landscape.
Little by little the field shuts down for the night
and the grass is grey, alive but not growing, flat in its hedgerows.
Flat between me and the last going-out of the going-out edge of
                                    the sky
stand nothing but outlines:

five tall trees with their backs turned, losing their branches,
black out of sight as the world gets less and less definite.
Every day ends something like this. Over a thickening inland sea
the last rook flaps uphill on its usual flight path
steering by farmlight.

To

This is no place to lie and stare
each last little light-loving insect
beats itself up to the window's star

the night, alive with lives to spare,
looks in at me awake in bed
I am its prisoner-of-war

the window's uncurtained squares-in-a-square,
from here as black as silhouette,
to eyes in the garden shine through bars.

Behind, I would climb down my hair
into sleep's steep-sided oubliette
I would not leave my head ajar

but let its thoughts rebreathe their air
until each knot of intellect
stopped fluttering. But here they are:

conscience moths, moths of despair
man moths I wish I could forget.
The window smiles on both sides of its glass

as they fracture their shoulders, snag and tear.
The garden quietly eats its dead
and blackout moths come to for more.

Cows

The cows would have nothing to do with me,
after a while they weren't even curious.
Whichever direction I came from I was the same
wrong thing, back again, impossible
to make head or tail of.
                         I liked to think I could see,
in their unhurried forward foraging across
the field, a sign that they did not complain.
They did not crowd the gate or jostle
their salt lick, but along the trail of shit
whose stink is all a cow can have of home
retraced their steps in search of missed sweet bits
with never a sideways look
                         and seemed content
to be kept in right up to the moment
they decided to leave
                         and then they went.

Thistles

Here I am again, at ease and out of sorts.
Because it's June the light is just the same,
the thistles are about as bright and tall,
as many (more!) and more or less arranged
the way they were last June, the June before,
and every June back to I don't know when.

Cutting them down is not so much a chore
as therapy endured to dull the brain,
the body's necessary pain absorbed
into a throbbing universe of green

where I am labourer and overlord,
the giant in his chapel and Gawain,
a sickle for my sword, the thistles thoughts
that seed from severed heads and rise again.

August

August again
in a house in the country

here comes my childhood
wheat beet and barley

run like the wind
my daughters love me

let's play pretend
we all have the same mummy

she's wearing her apron
and cooking spaghetti

nothing we do
can make her be happy

grassflowers camomile
speedwell and poppy

wilt on the windowsill
scatter their debris

leave me myself again
faint faded dusty

running the tap
as the kettle boils empty

somewhere in earshot
the children abruptly

look up from their game
remember they're thirsty.

Tapetum Lucidum

I

Sometimes the fields, sometimes the cows, change size.
Too strong a sun will push the fences back,
the open ground becomes an open eye,
the grass goes white, the lie of the land as flat
as overhead its blue unblinking sky,
the cows are pinprick rectangles of black

or slow cylindrical oil-storage tanks
that bump along together side by side,
eating themselves into the sunburnt bank
their blank exaggerated bodies hide.

Only a state of mind or trick of light,
I tell myself, but no less felt for that:
sometimes the cows, sometimes the fields, take fright,
the view foreshortens, thunderclouds close rank.

II

One day there was a new smell in the lab.
The bench was laid with cotton wool and knives.
We held our noses. Sir came round with eyes.

Cold and meaty, mine sat on its slab
and looked like someone trying not to cry.
Didn't I want to see the bright surprise

he promised lay behind its retina,
a picture of a black-as-midnight sky
alive with swirling turquoise butterflies?

I blinked away the salty abattoir
where quartered cattle hung in joints and sides
and washed my face and wiped my scalpel dry.

At night it's how the cows know where they are,
what catches in the headlights of a car.

III

Wait for it – the cows are about to disappear.
Half-solid half-imagined lines between
the black of what I can and cannot see
have kept me watching in the cold out here,

my pupils big as they will ever be,
more than an hour and now, though they are near,
the cows stand where my eyes can only hear,
ignoring their invisibility.

I have a herd of cattle in my ear!
Each one of them projects a double me
the wrong way up behind their dark corneas,

so small the little glow of blue and green
appears to throw its burning tapestry
of light across a northern hemisphere.

Cull

Three months of rain fell in an afternoon
the river rushed a fish farm upstream down

a hundred thousand rainbow trout set free
swam tail to fin in brown trout territory

tank-sick heron bait, scared of open water
run after run of them, layer on living layer

a lean omnivorous unsubsiding flood
that watched the sky and waited to be fed.

Pound by pound I pulled my own weight in silver
from a single pool, a catch a cast, the heavier

the harder to kill, one hand round the middle
a stone in the other, fish after fish, till

daylight was over, my twist of steel and feather
a stab in the dark, no way to save the river

the only way – tongue-torn, foul-hooked, half tame
when there was nothing more to take more came.

The Wood

I

Nothing special, a bit of old woodland
put to pine the same year I was born,
cut in the '90s, a square of stumps, then stakes,
and now this broadleaf native deciduous mix

bursting out of its plastic deer-proof bands
and solid with brambles, boisterous, immature,
left to establish, all the space
a canopy could need in reach of its leaf tips,

just a subsidy-funded timber stand
with rents and running costs accounted for
where birdsong and the light play tricks, a place
I go to let perspectives coexist,

look back from where I am at where I stood
and see the wood for the trees, the trees for the wood.

II

A kid on a quad bike stopped me in the wood.
He didn't know I'd been walking there for years,
so long it was my wood now, that crow my crow
beating in a wire cage on the road side.

I had to let him tell me where I stood
(lucky his boss, the Keeper, wasn't here!)
and feel him watch me have to turn and go
back to the public footpath, out of sight,

my feathered heart not beating as it should
but hard and wild as if my blood would tear
a hole to pour its boiling body through,
listening as the kid revved up his ride

behind me, trailer rattling, loaded with grain
and carrion, straw, a shovel and a gun.

III

There was a dog in the wood, a dog and then
a gun. Imagine, someone out shooting
in weather like this. Any minute, I thought,
it's going to come tearing through the undergrowth

and I will have to guess its intentions,
choosing very quickly *hand* or *boot*
or hope to be rescued, rescued and caught
again, walking where I'm not supposed.

There's more activity in there now than when
the children were children, I'm certain, though you
say I'm just imagining things. Of course,
why else do you think I'd choose to go

at twilight in the rain if not to listen
to my hairs on end, my senses trespassing?

Blackberries

It's dark by nine, stoats have been seen
on the dry stone wall by the sun-room,
and I have a feeling the blackberries need to be picked.

When I set off with my grandmother's hat, her stick and basket,
children run after me, thistles lie down,
the cows make way at the gate

and even the insects seem to disperse
more respectfully, leaving their eggs
in the crop's black best as if that might stop me

simmering the lot of them tomorrow
in the big aluminium pan. Somewhere in an outbuilding
jars of ten-year-old overboiled jam

recrystallise slowly (I should throw them away)
while the good stuff sits on a shelf in London
where no one has time for toast and tea.

No one else will put up with so many scratches,
wade into rosebay willowherb six foot high
or chance it with the stinging nettles,

bitten and burnt and aching all over,
filling the basket with little black blind spots,
berry-sized bruises that float in the eye.

This summer again, in patches of scrub
at the back of my mind, such fruit has been ripening
red from green and green from white

that somebody has to pick it, some sweet thing
of the sweetness of August's August rain
be preserved.

Down

We stripped the beds and took our luggage down.
The car was waiting for us in the sun.
Somewhere a tractor stuttered up and down.
Next week all the stubble would be gone.

From Macclesfield to Chesterfield and down
along the smooth spectacular M1
we sat in weight of traffic weighted down
with going back to where we started from,

a mile for every mile the sun went down
until we had to turn the headlights on
and let the yellow fields turn upside down,

the breathless, bruised, uprooted night begin
its nightly atmospheric rotting down
that closed around the car and pressed us in.

III

By the River Lau

In Mino by the river Lau
there lived the artisan
who pressed and dried the pulp that made
an origami man.

Like onion silk her gampi paper
crackled in the air
long-fibred fine as a sheet of light
a single shining square

she held between her fingertips
and folded in her mind
until she had by heart a map
of intersecting lines.

Then she closed her eyes, breathed in
and leaning on both hands
pinched and pleated bone by bone
an origami man.

Between her fingertips he lay
beneath a paper sky
the glimmer of a thought behind
his glossy onion eyes

and as she looked the laughter lines
across his face uncreased
the concertina chest drew in
she saw her masterpiece

roll over yawning, stretch and sigh
and fall asleep again
to dream within his thumbnail folds
the dreams of life-sized men.

Hours she watched him, light slipped through
the mesh between the frames
that leant in every corner waiting
slowly darkness came.

Darkness settled, still she watched
and what she couldn't see
she felt, a flutter in her ear
how quietly he breathed.

How quietly the river raced
between the bamboo stands;
she held her breath and listened to
the rivers in her hands.

She watched him as the silkscreen dawn
arrived in squares of grey
as strips of sunlight slanted in
and lit him where he lay

asleep, but not as she had seen
him sleep the night before
a poor, imperfect, woman-made
man shape was all she saw

an onion-coloured paper doll
no better folded than
a thousand figures folded by
a thousand artisans.

She turned him over, picked him up
between her fingertips
and ran her nail along his spine
and folded back his hips.

She didn't feel him buck and twist
but pulled his ribs apart
to watch the palpitations of
his pleated paper heart.

Limb by limb she opened him
till fluttering in her hand
she held the creases of an empty
wrapping paper plan

a map, a landscape, patchwork plains,
a maze of broken lines
cross-hatched according to her own
impossible design.

She squinted through that square of skin
and black against the sun
a tiny shattered skeleton
revealed what she had done

and then she knew however many
papers she began
she'd never bring to life another
origami man.

In Mino people still recall
the night her house burnt down.
They say she set herself alight
but in the ash they found

no human char or shred or shard
no bitter black remains
only the burnt off corners of
her paper-making frames

and when they gather gampi bark
above the bamboo stands
sometimes a crumpled figure holding
something in her hands

steps out of nowhere, face by face
begs anyone who can
to fold her ragged scrap of paper
back into a man.

My Hand

I had just turned to face the door,
as usual I slept, you read,
when in a quiet voice you said
you never touch me any more.

At once I reached across the bed
but reaching felt my hand withdraw –
how many nights had I ignored
your tics and twitches, sighs and sweats

and woken shivering at dawn
my hip against the mattress edge?
The duvet held its double breath,
the pillows could not say for sure

how many nights I had instead
dismissed as a domestic chore
the tenderness we shared before,
too flat to let myself be led

across the undulating floor
of hand-me-down parquet bedspread
Granny salvaged shred by shred
in threadbare 1944,

sick of margarine and bread
and tired of waiting on the war,
of telegrams in pinafores
and bogeymen in garden sheds,

picturing in scraps of cardboard,
khaki strips and squares of red,
a soldier's decorated chest,
the overcoat her husband wore.

I looked at you and as you slept
my body, suddenly too warm,
remembered what its blood was for,
my fingers tingled with regret

and reached a second time towards
your folded arms and open neck.
My lips were dry, my face was wet,
but when I closed my eyes I saw

something in me not ready yet
to let me let you rest assured,
and made my hand a human claw
and clenched the air above your head.

no handkerchief   not even a proper tissue
just a wadge of emergency bog paper
I must have pocketed in someone's bathroom
when the children were young   do you remember
this was the only jacket I would wear
the little hole my change kept falling through
still wants a stitch   and after all these years
here is the same already   sorry   used
disintegrating papier mâché bloom
its scrunch of perforated pastel squares
dry now   of course   but possible to smooth
or fiddle gently   see?   back into shape
in an emergency   its crust of tears
perhaps the last good cry I had of you
a salty   near invisible   remainder
if you need it   it will have to do

Between Our Feet

What's going on between our feet?
Once they only came along
because they liked to make us wait,
dragging their heels to demonstrate
their own stand-offish distance from
the moments we arranged to meet.

Now they kick their shoes off early,
twenty sweaty toes insist
on carrying us up to bed.
Prehensile, uninhibited
their arches lift and ankles twist,
they make us blush above the knee

remembering the supple stuff
we were, our human leather soft
and sensitive as lengths of suede,
before we let ourselves abrade
on nights of fitted, thin white cloth.
We lie as if we've had enough,

with only the cool well-trodden skin
of our footprints touching, sole to sole.
Our insteps rest their featherweight
as if they know they incubate
something I want to call our soul,
alive and fluttering within

as it gets ready to unfold
the precarious expanding mesh
of its first full breath into the wings
you'd hope for of a made-up thing,
trembling, ticklish and compressed
as love should be, losing its foothold.

Look

Now I know what I look like
how much easier it is
to spot myself in daily life
going about my daily business.

Look: I'm sitting in a car
I'm running down the escalator
kissing in a cinema
I'm on the pavement with a letter.

I can see I'm far too busy
to observe our passing likeness,
only one of us need be
the one the other recognises

and these grubby jeans,
my favourites, these unpolished shoes
are not the size or shape of thing
someone who looks like her would choose.

(How ought she to look who knows
it makes no difference what she wears
she never seems to suit her clothes
the colour of her skin or hair,

if not in tissue, blood and bone
as indeterminate as me:
surrounded, flickering, alone
exceptional and ordinary?)

Magnified we are the same
and from a distance. In my mind
imagining a stranger's pain
the pain I feel is pain in kind

but when she smiles her happiness
materialises in my brain,
it is her face my face projects
and for a moment I look strange.

One

Left in the house
to play all morning
solitaire

little glass men
as round as the grid
their world is square

over they hop
or else hopped over
disappear

block by block
their cities empty
roads are clear

knots of survivors
pull together
tooth and claw

under my feet
their fallen grind
the dusty floor

they can't put
my lunch on the table
light a fire

or tell me again
the picture book riches
of an empire

mine for the loss
of all but my last
glass-hearted player

standing apart
from the rest, a shining
knight in prayer

who waits his turn
wishing
he was not there.

My Heart

My heart got up unexpectedly one night
and went out drinking and dancing and spending its money.
All I could do was hold my breath and look at my eyelids.
All I could feel was blood not moving in my veins.

Thirsty, pink as candyfloss collecting on a stick
my heart went bumping into things on purpose,
throwing its lightness about and falling over lavishly.
Anything stupid it did to make people laugh.

There wasn't a care in the world it could refuse.
It grew so full of itself I thought the hole in my chest
would empty the room like a red hot-air balloon,
pumping the chair to the wall and flattening bed-springs.

Knick-knacks cracked at the window as my heart
drove by in a minicab looking for other emotions,
still not big enough yet to body me for a change,
come home with its head in its hands and hold me tight.

Between

Stuck in your car
in the dark winter rush hour tailback red
you forget what you're wearing

your skin is the colour of nothing there
your body knows where you have been
but it isn't telling

all you can do is sit in your weight
in your breathing space
bumper to bumper breathing

London at night is a blaze of company
people you love
continue their evenings

the car pulls up
but sometimes you keep your seat belt on
and the engine running.

Two

Into my room, the low-pitched frequency
of a fly in December, too excited
to settle down and be killed just yet,

its blue-black baritone figure-of-eight
a shoulder-height attic-shaped song of dimensions
spun to the light I went on reading by

or would have when a second fly, a greenbottle
quick on its wings, came in five semitones up
with the tune from some late night winter fly duet.

Over the bed they flew in close disharmony,
under and through each other's vibrato,
sound in their hair and the scent

in their chemoreceptors of something on me
that warmed their insect-blooded hearts
with insect pleasure.

Next Door

Next door they too experience life to the full.
They have the usual useful household stuff,
their shelves and kitchen cabinets are full.

Room by room they're doing the place up,
as if to make themselves more beautiful
by colouring the walls some shade they love

but it's the same old street outside, cheerful
and foul, the same run-down rough
neighbourhood: bins are always full

in people's front gardens, drains and gutters flood,
the silt between the paving stones is full
of shit, the playground saturated mud,

its silver sky reflected still and full
in every soggy bootprint. On his rug
their stocky dog squeezes a full lungful

of solid indoor air across the gulp
at the back of his throat as if to stuff it full
and howls until the walls have had enough.

Under their paint even the cracks fill full
of tiny flecks of settled man-made dust,
each with a tale to tell, a story full

of noisy unintended human rub,
the bang and slam of lives lived to the full
a nine-inch party wall apart from us.

Cento

All the trees that are in the wood
are wrapped in swathing bands
heat is in the very sod
and thorns infest the ground

Snow has fallen, snow on snow
mountains in reply
sing gloria in excelsis deo
silent ships go by

Fast away the old year passes
Christmas comes once more
dressed in gay apparel lasses
beg from door to door

Poor boys shelter by the fence
gathering winter fuel
heedless of the wind's lament
the holly decks the hall

Brightly shines the morning star
by prophet bards foretold
after the running of the deer
shall come the age of gold

Night will break and glory shake
the rising of the sun
the old familiar carols play
pa rum pum pum pum

call it what you like
                         but when we stop
on a B-road high over steep late winter Exmoor
where a few poor spray-painted lambs
already suckle in the wind and we
are the only tourists suddenly
                              when we stop
and I look up as if to see what for

you leaping out through a blast of land to stand
as men on boats stand in the sea
fighting for breath   the quick acoustic shock
of open air slammed shut   your empty door
the view through your window

                         I make what I can
an old black bin bag snagged on wire
noisily tearing itself to shreds without a sound
the other side of the force in the fence
                              of the foreground

Acknowledgements

Thank you to the editors of *Ambit, Magma, New Welsh Review, Poetry London, Poetry Review, Poetry Wales,* the *Spectator,* the *TLS,* and the *Warwick Review,* where many of these poems were originally published.

I'm grateful to the poets in the North London Monday workshop, the Thurlow Road workshop, and the National Theatre workshop whose poetry and criticism have been so sustaining over the years.

Thanks also to everyone at Seren, and to my editor Amy Wack in particular for her tact and patience. And finally to my husband whose advice was inspired.

Notes

'On Highgate Hill' follows 'We Field-Women' by Thomas Hardy.

'Midnight' follows 'Stopping By Woods On A Snowy Evening' by Robert Frost.

'Cento' is a collage of lines from Christmas carols.